Our Animal World

Animal Tracks

by Karen Latchana Kenney

amicus readers 1

Say hello to amicus readers.

You'll find our helpful dog, Amicus, chasing a ball—to let you know the reading level of a book.

Learn to Read	**Read Independently**	**Read to Know More**
Frequent repetition of sentence structures, high frequency words, and familiar topics provide ample support for brand new readers. Approximately 100 words.	Repetition is mixed with varied sentence structures and 6 to 8 content words per book are introduced with photo label and picture glossary supports. Approximately 150 words.	These books feature a higher text load with additional nonfiction features such as more photos, time lines, and text divided into sections. Approximately 250 words.

Amicus Readers are published by **Amicus**
P.O. Box 1329, Mankato, Minnesota 56002

Series Editor	Rebecca Glaser
Book Editor	Wendy Dieker
Series Designer	Kia Adams
Book Designer	Heather Dreisbach
Photo Researcher	Heather Dreisbach

Printed in the United States of America at
Corporate Graphics, in North Mankato, Minnesota.

1022
3-2011

10 9 8 7 6 5 4 3 2 1

Library of Congress Cataloging-in-Publication Data
Kenney, Karen Latchana.
  Animal tracks / by Karen Latchana Kenney.
    p. cm. – (Amicus readers. Our animal world)
  Includes index.
  Summary: "A Level 1 Amicus Reader that describes different kinds of animals' tracks. Examples show that by looking at the parts of animal tracks, you can tell what animal left them behind. Includes comprehension activity"–Provided by publisher.
  ISBN 978-1-60753-142-5 (library binding)
  1. Animal tracks–Juvenile literature. I. Title.
QL768.K46 2011
591.47'9–dc22
                                      2010033480

Table of Contents

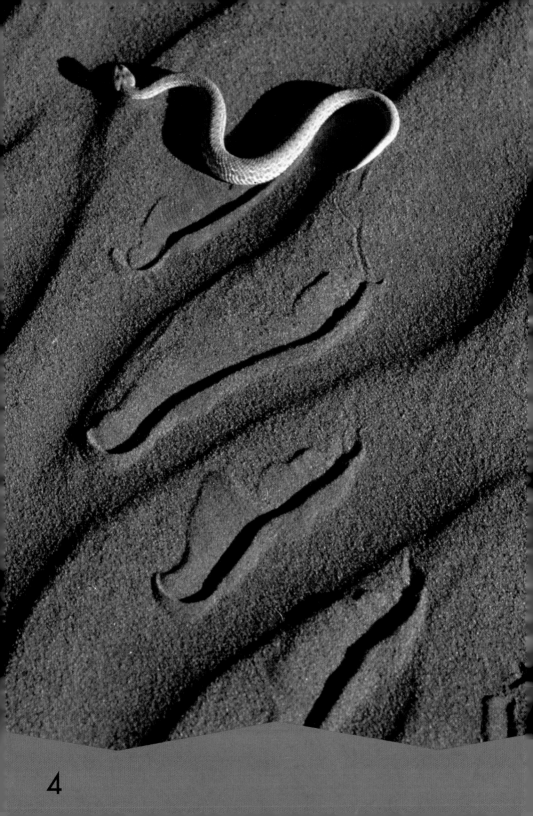

As animals move, tracks are left behind. A row of j-shapes in the sand shows a sidewinder snake was there.

A deer's hoof leaves a track with two parts. It is shaped like a heart. The points show where the deer went.

hoof

Raccoon tracks are made with five long toes. Each toe has a sharp claw. The tracks look like tiny human hands.

claw

Ducks live near water. They leave their tracks in the mud. Their webbed feet leave marks between their toes.

webbed feet

11

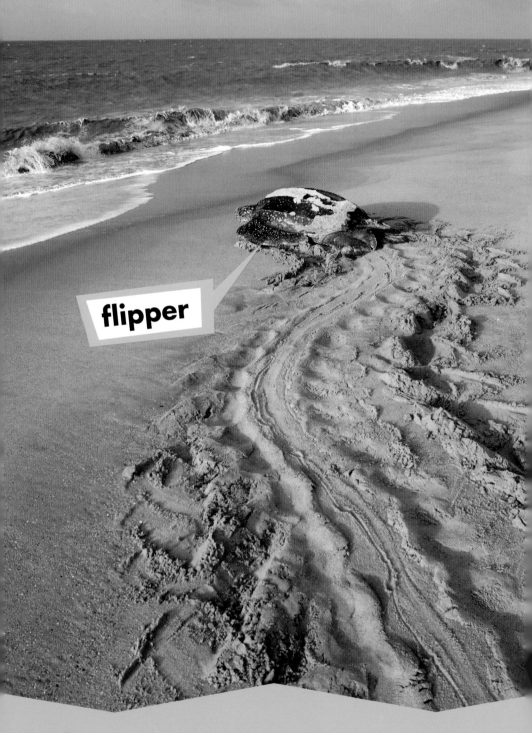

flipper

A sea turtle's tracks look like a tire made them. The turtle drags its heavy body with its four flippers.

Polar bears leave tracks as wide as a dinner plate. Their huge paws help them walk on ice and snow.

paws

A hopping rabbit leaves its tracks behind. Its long hind feet land just in front of its round front feet.

hind feet

Just like animals, tracks come in all shapes and sizes. Take a look at your footprints. What do you see?

claws
the hard, curved nails
of animals and birds

flipper
a flat limb of a
sea animal

hind feet
the back feet of
an animal

20

hoof
the hard end of a
horse or deer foot

paw
an animal's foot that
has claws and pads

webbed feet
feet that have a
fold of skin between
the toes

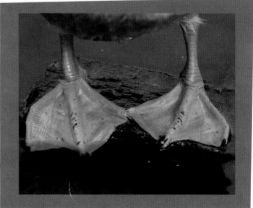

21

What Do You Remember?

Match each animal to its track.

If you don't remember, read through
the book again for the answers.

Ideas for Parents and Teachers

Our Animal World, an Amicus Readers Level 1 series, gives children fascinating facts about animals with ample reading support. In each book, photo labels and a picture glossary reinforce new vocabulary. The activity page reinforces comprehension and critical thinking. Use the ideas below to help children get even more out of their reading experience.

Before Reading

- Look at the cover of the book. Ask students to discuss what they think the book will be about.
- Find out what students already know about animal tracks.
- Discuss what students want to learn about animal tracks.

During Reading

- Read the book to students or have them read independently.
- Take a picture walk through the book. Ask students to describe what they see.
- After each spread, ask students to write a sentence about what they learned.

After Reading

- Ask students to look at page 22 and match the animals to the tracks they make.
- Discuss what each track tells about the animal that made it.
- Ask students to describe the tracks they've seen in nature.

Index

Web Sites

BioKids: Tracks and Sign Guide
http://www.biokids.umich.edu/guides/tracks_and_sign/

Environmental Education for Kids: Follow That Footprint,
Paw Print, Hoof Print ...
http://www.dnr.state.wi.us/org/caer/ce/eek/nature/track.htm

NBII Kids Animal Tracks
http://kids.nbii.gov/tracks.html